I DON'T KNOW
❖ HOW ❖
TO HELP THEM

BY LINDA K. MAURER

Second Printing, 1996
Library of Congress Catalog Card Number 96-94092
Copyright © 1993 by Linda K. Maurer
ISBN 0-9636977-2-2

Linda K. Maurer
7386 Buckingham Court
Boulder, CO 80301-6413

Printed by Johnson Printing, Boulder, Colorado

TABLE OF CONTENTS

This book is dedicated with love to the many friends and family members who have helped us survive the worst year of our lives. You know who you are and no words can adequately thank you.

I would also like to thank Reverend John Hess and Leslie Conger of the First Presbyterian Church, Boulder, Colorado, for their encouragement and assistance in preparing this book for publication.

In Memory

MOLLY MARIE MAURER

10-13-71   3-16-91

ACHIEVEMENT

That woman is a success who has lived well, laughed often and loved much; who has gained the respect of intelligent men and the love of children; who has filled her niche and accomplished her task; who leaves the world better than she found it, whether by an improved poppy, a perfect poem or a rescued soul; who never lacked appreciation of earth's beauty or failed to express it; who looked for the best in others and gave the best she had.

Robert Louis Stevenson

Introduction

I am not a psychiatrist, a psychologist, or a grief counselor. I am not, by profession, a writer. I am simply a bereaved parent who lost her only child in a tragic accident on March 16, 1991. Our daughter, Molly, was 19½ years old.

Since that time, people with friends who have lost children have come to me in great frustration and said, "I don't know how to help them."

Because losing a child is the worst of all tragedies, people simply do not know what to do—how to help—what to say and not to say.

As friends, you honestly hurt for the bereaved parents. You want, more than anything, to take away their pain. Your heart aches for them. You cry for them and with them. You, too, miss the child that has been suddenly taken away from them.

What should you do for them immediately—what should you do for them in the weeks and months ahead?

This book was written for you, friends of bereaved parents. I believe it can offer you valuable ideas and suggestions. Believe me when I say that your friend needs you now more than ever.

L.M.
Boulder, Colorado
June, 1992

Before Their Time

Our children are only given to us
for just a little while.
They give us joy, they make us cry,
and most often make us smile.

We watch them grow and we watch them go
and we hope life will be kind.
And we try to help as they travel along
with a fear in the back of our mind.

We always fear the "FEAR" of fears
avoid it though we try
that one of our children before their time
will be the first to die.

And then it happens, that awful thing,
the thing that should never be;
and we look for some kind of meaning
though it is hard for us to see.

For life is not the thing we thought
and not the things we plan.
And as we face what happened here,
we do the best we can.

We stare into your tear-stained eyes
and try to hug your pain,
because we know the one that died
might well have had our name.

It's so unfair to be left behind
to feel this pain of death
But there are others to share that pain
and feel it with each breath.

We want to do things that we can do
to try and lighten the load.
Everyone needs friends and family
on a long and painful road.

Don't we all wish we could change it
and have the power to give
a new ending to the story
and somehow let them live.

Don't we wish that we could take their place
and shield them from the pain;
and though we know we can't do that
we keep wishing just the same.

Don't you wish we would have done something
to have stopped it with one hand;
and maybe it wouldn't have happened
if we only had time to plan.

But just maybe this is a better plan
and maybe it does make sense
I somehow think that is true
and not just blind pretense.

Maybe this will set them free
to be where they should be.
Maybe this is what is best
though it is hard on you and me.

They say that for every door that closes
another opens up.
And so it seems we must pass through
with what seems like an emptied cup.

But the cup holds more than memories
it has a strength within
and with your faith and family
it will be filled again.

And those who went before us,
though we hate to see them going,
have found a place that is nice and safe
and their cup is overflowing.

For life is more than what we think;
it's more than what we plan.
It takes a lot of loving and hope
and doing the best we can.

Our children are only given to us
and we do love them so
but the hardest of hards and the saddest of sads
is to somehow let them go.

George Ray Russell, M.D.
Boulder, Colorado, 1990

CHAPTER ONE

The Immediate Needs of the Bereaved

Molly was a freshman at Arizona State University. She and friends from her dormitory planned a spring break trip to Mazatlan, Mexico, arranged through a local Phoenix travel agency. They were to travel by way of Mexican train. On Saturday morning, March 16, 1991, Molly and three of her friends drove to Nogales, Mexico and boarded the train at approximately 3:30 P.M.

My husband, Larry, and I had just returned from lunch on Sunday afternoon when we received the first phone call. The man was a parent of one of Molly's friends who was travelling with the group. He had received a call from his daughter saying that Molly was missing and may have fallen off the train. Having thought that trains were the safest means of transportation, we were shocked and stunned. He proceeded to give us the telephone numbers where we could personally talk with her friends, as well as the American Consulate's office.

Upon reaching Molly's friends who were now in Mazatlan, we realized how grave the situation really was. They told us Molly had fallen from the train at approximately 9:30 P.M. on Saturday evening. The Mexican train employees refused to stop the train and search for Molly, forcing her friends to continue on for another fifteen hours into Mazatlan not knowing the fate of their friend. Those young people were in a state of hysteria as they related to us the details of the previous night.

We then contacted the American Consulate's office, who informed us that a search for Molly was in progress and they would get back with us as soon as possible.

With a pounding heart and uncontrollable panic building within me, I called my brother and sister-in-law to relate the story and told them we needed help. Larry then called his brother to notify the Maurer family members. Banks, of course, are closed on Sundays; therefore, we called various friends to bring whatever cash they might have available. Another friend arranged for a private plane to fly us to the closest town where Molly was estimated to have fallen. We were packed and ready to leave. Our sister-in-law called the American Consulate's office in Hermosillo to inform them that we were on our way to aid in the search. We heard her say, "What body!" She then screamed and handed the phone to someone else standing in the kitchen. Molly's body had been found.

By this time, there were several family members and friends gathered in our home. Tears of pain mingled with the silence of shock filled the house. Larry and I had become bereaved parents. We had lost the joy of our lives, our best friend, our reason for living and breathing, and our future. Molly was our only child.

From that point on, and for the duration of the week to come, our friends and family took over our existence. Larry and I were totally helpless, suffering from pain so deep and severe that no words could possibly describe it.

As Friends, What Do We Do First?

Ask the bereaved parents if they wish to contact other friends and family members themselves or if they would prefer for someone else to make the calls.

Determine if a doctor or minister needs to be contacted for the parents or other family members.

Take it upon yourselves to call the obvious friends. Then sit down with one or both of the parents and go through an address book to find out who should be contacted. Have a pad and pencil ready to make a list of the names. If there are quite a few people to be contacted, divide the list up with another friend. As long as there are plenty of people to stay with the bereaved family, go to your separate homes to make these calls. This will free up the family's own phone for incoming calls.

Delegate someone to buy legal size notepads and pencils. You will need them during the entire week for many reasons.

The bereaved parents will not want to answer the phone. Someone should be available at all times to man the phone and take messages. For those people who wish to talk directly with the mother or father, check first with them to see if they wish to take the call.

That first night, after most of the people had gone home, two friends and two family members spent the night with us. Sleep did not come until the early hours of the morning. We needed to talk and our friends and family members were there for us. At least two friends spent the nights with us until after the funeral. Not only were they company for us after the crowds of the day had left, but they were there to answer the early morning phone calls and to make coffee. A new crew of friends arrived each morning to relieve those who had spent the night so that they could go home to shower and rest.

Friends did our laundry, picked up our dry cleaning and changed our sheets and towels. As flowers and food started to arrive, lists were begun stating the type of plant or flowers sent and from whom, as well as the many food items which were brought. These lists proved very useful down the road, not only for the purpose of "thank you" notes, but by reading them, Larry and I realized just how many people sincerely cared about us.

As friends, you need to arrange meals. Food and beverages need to be available at all times, for people come and go all day and all night. Many of our friends would call or come by every morning and get a list of needed items for the day. Suggested items are: toilet paper, Kleenex, paper plates and cups, plastic glasses, coffee, napkins, paper towels, plastic wrap, foil, Baggies, stick-on food labels, dish-washing detergent, hand soap, soda pop and liquor.

Cleaning the House

One of our friends took it upon herself to clean our house each morning, and often again at night. Another friend religiously took home the dining room tablecloth each night, laundered it, and returned it the next morning. The morning we left for the funeral, a maid service was hired to prepare the house for the gathering afterwards. It might be a good idea for a maid service to be hired also for the day after the funeral.

How You Can Help with Funeral Arrangements

A funeral home, a casket and a cemetery plot must be selected as soon as possible. A friend should be chosen to accompany the bereaved parents and/or family members. Preferably this friend should be one who is a good business person and has a mind for details. Our friend who accompanied us had with him a notepad and pen with which to take notes at both the funeral home and the cemetery. Bereaved parents more often than not will know what they want, but cannot handle or concentrate on the financial details.

Our daughter's funeral was held at First Presbyterian Church in our hometown of Boulder, Colorado. We had not been active members of the church for some time. However, Larry's sister, and a couple of friends who are all members of the church, personally contacted their favorite minister, Reverend John Hess. He agreed to do the service. They told him about us and about Molly. He then arranged a time to visit our home and make final arrangements with us. We were grateful they made the initial contact on our behalf.

The bereaved parents most likely will want and need to be very involved in the funeral arrangements as well as the program for the service. However, they do need your help with details and organization. In our case, we knew that our friends, as well as Molly's peers, should be involved in the actual service. As a friend, find out what the parents have in mind and help them follow through. Biblical passages or other spiritual readings need to be selected, songs must be determined, pallbearers notified, and so on. Make sure a friend or acquaintance will be staying at the bereaved parent's home during the time of the funeral.

Larry's sister suggested that balloons be passed out to everyone attending the services at the cemetery. When the minister had concluded his final prayer, he announced that everyone could either keep their balloons or release them. Larry and I stood up at that point, and looking upward toward the blue sky, released our balloons. Within seconds the sky was full of beautiful balloons floating upward to the heavens. It was quite a mystical sight; peacefully and serenely, people stood in silence and prayer and watched until the last balloon was out of sight.

Special friends of ours living in Phoenix, along with Molly's college roommate, packed up her belongings from her dorm room. They stored the boxes until such time that we were ready to have them shipped. They, along with their son, provided Molly's Arizona State friends with transportation to the Phoenix airport. Friends here in Boulder arranged for discounted airline fares for these students. As Molly's friends and our friends began arriving at the Denver airport, people at our home alternated trips to the airport. Boulder friends generously offered their homes to our out-of-state friends, as well as the college students. Many of the Arizona State friends stayed in our home, and a kind neighbor graciously gave us her house keys so that everyone could shower and be ready *on time* the morning of the funeral.

Viewing the Deceased Child

Parents may or may not want to view the body of their deceased child. If a child dies in a terrible accident, as our child did, one or both of the parents may choose to remember the child as before. In our case, my husband very much wanted and needed to see Molly, and I chose not to do so. It is a very personal decision each parent must make, whether they regret it later or not. Very dear friends, as well as Larry's sister, went to the funeral home and changed Molly's lip color and bought a hat to cover a bad wound on her face. This was a difficult and yet loving display of affection. My husband and those who chose to view Molly were most grateful to these caring individuals. Photographs of the lovely hat were taken for me.

As you can see, there are so many ways in which friends can help. Even with the shock and devastation of the moment, our friends' love and generosity are remembered by both Larry and me, never, never to be forgotten.

CHAPTER TWO

What to do in the weeks and months following the funeral

Though my husband and I were exhausted from the week of shock, pain, disbelief and very little sleep, we were not totally ready to be alone. Friends continued to fix us lunch and dinner for quite a while, sharing the meals with us. We needed to talk and they were there to listen.

Returning to Jobs

Returning to a job is the first step in returning to routine life, and it is a most difficult step. If you are a friend of the bereaved parent who has the time, offer to drive him or her to and from work for the first few days. Driving requires concentration and bereaved people have a hard time concentrating on anything in the early stages of grief.

If you are a co-worker of the bereaved, you can be very helpful. The ability of a person in mourning to comprehend or concentrate, as mentioned, is at an all-time low: offer to assist him/her in whatever way you can. What may have been "routine responsibilities" two weeks ago, will now seem like insurmountable tasks to the grieving parent resuming a job.

The Parent at Home

I had quit my job previous to Molly's death. When Larry returned to his job full time, the days could have been long and lonely. However, friends called every morning to see if they could come by to talk, take me to lunch or simply drive me to the bank, the cleaners, or run other such errands. Special friends had a schedule of sorts giving each of them the free time they needed, but still making sure that I was not alone if I didn't want to be. Do be aware that the bereaved parent will not only want some time alone, but will need time alone. Do not smother your friend; rather, let her know that you are always there if she needs you.

As a friend, know that some normal, everyday tasks are very difficult for at least three to four weeks. Among those, some of the most difficult for me were shopping at the neighborhood grocery or buying needed items at the local mall or department store. By keeping in daily touch with your friend, you can find out what she needs and take care of it for her.

Talking about the Deceased Child

The bereaved parents need to talk about their deceased child—not just the good times, but often the details of his/her death. This will not be easy for you, but do the best you can to listen and to contribute your own thoughts and feelings of love and pain.

Letters and Flowers

For many months after Molly's death, we continued receiving greeting cards and beautifully written notes and letters. Flowers also were sent sporadically by caring friends. These gestures, long after Molly's death, meant so much to Larry and me. It relayed to us that people were still thinking of us, and that they understood and accepted that the pain of losing a child is forever.

The Child's Belongings

Going through a deceased child's room—drawers, closets, bathroom—is by far one of the most difficult of all chores. Offer to help your friend. Some bereaved parents may want to tackle this alone; others may want your help. Don't rush them. They will know when the time is right. I, personally, chose to go through each drawer myself over a period of weeks. Some days, I could only handle one drawer before the tears started to fall, but I did finally finish the task.

Most of Molly's belongings, however, were in her dorm room at the time of her death. Those boxes were shipped from Phoenix to a friend's home here in Boulder shortly after the funeral. Four months after Molly's death, when Larry and I felt up to it, the boxes were brought to our home. With fifteen of Molly's friends and a couple of our friends present, we slowly and painfully opened the boxes. Larry and I kept a few items, then allowed her friends to have whatever they wanted. It was a terrible day, but sharing it with our friends and Molly's friends made it a lot easier to handle. It was another difficult step behind us.

Social Life

Try to help your friends resume their normal social life. This will have to be done very slowly. Have your friends for a quiet dinner in your home or go out for an early dinner at a restaurant. Be prepared for tears in public. It will happen for a long time. Keep social gatherings to small groups—two, three or four couples. Bereaved parents will probably stay away from larger parties for quite some time. Help them return to their favorite sports—golf, tennis, bowling, skiing, fishing, or just walking. Exercise is very important and helps to eliminate some of the stress and depression. In time, you will gradually see your friends improve—even laugh sometimes.

Books and Groups

Buy your friends books about grief. Any book store can help you select the appropriate ones. Reading books written by parents who have survived the loss of a child gives hope and encouragement to the newly bereaved.

Meeting with other bereaved parents in organized groups can be very helpful, as pain and grief can be shared with those who truly understand. Bereavement groups, however, are not for everyone, and many parents prefer individual therapy.

Following the last chapter of this book, you will find a list of organized grief groups, as well as suggested reading material.

Helpful Gifts

Give your bereaved friend a journal to write in. A friend of Molly's gave me one a couple of weeks after her death. As I was accustomed to writing letters to Molly at college, the journal enabled me to continue doing so. I wrote of my feelings, my fears, my love for her, and eventually of our daily activities. As men often have a more difficult time verbally expressing their grief, I strongly suggest a journal for the bereaved father, as well. I have just recently given Larry a journal and he feels that it is a valuable tool for healing. My regret is that it was not given to him sooner.

Another nice gift is a candle. One of the grief books I read after Molly's death suggested buying a candle to light during the holidays in memory of the deceased child. I bought a large candle for Larry and me, but not just for the holiday time. We light it any time that we feel sad, and always during our evening meal. It seems to give us comfort that though she is not here physically, her spirit is always with us.

Don't Push

Do not try to rush or put a timetable on your bereaved friends' grief. Don't judge how they are handling their grief. Trust that they as individuals are doing the best they can. Each person handles grief differently. Encourage them to take just one day at a time. They may not deal with their grief in the same manner you would, but at least they are coping as well as can be expected.

Last but not least, don't be afraid to cry with your bereaved friends. Your tears only say that you also loved their child, and that you openly share in their grief.

CHAPTER THREE

What can you do when you live too far away?

When informed of the death of your friend's child, you may or may not attend the funeral. Your friend may suggest that you wait for a visit later when fewer people are around.

Whether you attend the funeral or not, you now find yourself many miles from your bereaved friend. You obviously will call, write letters, send cards and perhaps flowers occasionally. What else?

Plan a trip to visit as soon and as often as you can. Ask your friend when it would be convenient to schedule your trip.

Plan a vacation with your bereaved friends. Remember that any holiday—Mother's Day, Father's Day, even their own birthdays are very difficult. If possible, plan a trip with them to coincide with just such an occasion.

The bereaved parents probably will not want to travel to any of the same vacation areas where they have taken their child—at least not in the first year. The best trips are those that offer plenty of activity, whether it is golf, tennis, fishing, or camping. Larry and I found Las Vegas to be ideal because there is plenty of activity, and you really never know what time it is or sometimes even what day it is when you are inside the casinos.

My college roommate and her husband visited us about a month after Molly's death. Not only was it wonderful to have them here, but they were a tremendous help in organizing contributions that had come in the mail. They separated them by charity organization, removed the cash and personal checks from envelopes, and organized a list for "thank you" notes. Most of all, just knowing they traveled such a distance to see us displayed their love and concern for us. Bereaved parents need to know they are loved.

Seven months after Molly's death, another friend came from Indianapolis, my home town. Her husband had passed away three months after Molly. As we had not seen each other in years, we had a great deal to talk about. We planned some activities, but mostly consoled one another.

Friends from Chicago met us in Las Vegas for New Year's Eve. It helped so much not only to be out of town, but also to be with friends who cared. Bringing in the new year would have been very difficult had Larry and I been alone.

In other words, though you cannot be with your bereaved friends on a day-to-day basis, you can be of tremendous help in many different and rewarding ways.

CHAPTER FOUR

Thoughtful things to do at the cemetery

Before our daughter's death, I had not given much thought to cemeteries and their possible importance. Molly's grave has become a place of peace and contentment—a place to think about her and silently talk with her. In other words, it can be a very special place for the bereaved parents and you, as a friend, can share this with them.

It will normally take two to three months after ordering a headstone for it to be completed and installed at the grave site. For some reason, it was hard for Larry and I to go there without something in place to designate Molly's grave. Larry's brother ordered a temporary headstone made of sandstone with Molly's name engraved on it. It was only 2' by 2', but it was such a wonderful gift. The temporary stone made a difference not only to us but also to other family members and friends. Sometimes the funeral home will make a temporary marker of some sort, but not normally.

If your bereaved friends like going to the cemetery, offer to go with them. It can be a wonderful place to communicate, to pray, to cry together. Before Molly's friends returned to their various colleges in the fall, they suggested we have a picnic together at the grave. Everyone brought their own sandwiches and soda pop and we sat around the grave and talked about our grief, our hopes for the future and our memories of Molly.

On her birthday in October, our friends and family members, along with the minister and his family, met at the cemetery. People brought flowers, balloons and small gifts; together we wished Molly a Happy

Birthday. Reverend Hess offered a wonderful prayer as we all encircled the headstone and held hands. Afterwards we came back to our house for dinner where more friends joined us and we celebrated the life of our child. Everyone contributed food pot-luck style and Molly's friends who attend college locally joined us. Her friends needed to be with us on this sad occasion as much as we needed to be with them. Though the day was terribly painful for Larry and me, our friends and family helped us through with their love and support.

Suggest to your bereaved friends that a tree be planted by their child's grave if this would be permitted by the owners of the cemetery. We also have two vases on Molly's headstone for fresh flowers in the summer and silk flowers in the winter. The silk flowers, even here in Colorado with the cold temperatures and snow, made it through beautifully this past winter. During the summer months many friends, Molly's friends, and family members brought fresh flowers to her grave.

At Christmas, we decorated Molly's tree at the cemetery, and a close friend made a beautiful fresh wreath on which people tied ornaments with their names inscribed. Someone else, anonymously, had a large fresh wreath placed behind Molly's headstone on a stand. It means a great deal to bereaved parents to see flowers, ornaments or any thoughtful gift brought to their child's grave, because it means other people miss her and love her and are still thinking of their precious child who is no longer here.

CHAPTER FIVE

Suggestions for the holidays and other special occasions

The first holiday after Molly's death was Easter. Larry and I found that we could not be with either one of our families because Molly's absence would be so obvious. We chose rather to have a quiet dinner with friends who understood our feelings about normal family gatherings on Easter Sunday.

Mother's Day was soon to follow and I will never forget the pain that preceded that day. The beautiful child who had made me a mother was now gone. I would never again receive a Mother's Day card from her—never again hear her say, "I love you, Mom."

Once again, friends came through. Several couples planned a cookout and invited Molly's friends as well. Her friends called me "Mom" like always and gave me a very special group picture of all of them, including Molly, taken the summer before they all left for college. Though everyone there was still very much in pain and disbelief, the gathering was upbeat.

Father's Day was as difficult for Larry as Mother's Day had been for me. Our neighborhood friends planned a small cookout at their home. Before going to their home, Molly's wonderful friends came to our house and brought Larry a gift and beautiful card signed by all of them. We made it through another tough one!

Larry's 50th birthday followed in June and was spent only with adult members of his family. Having the other grandchildren there without Molly, the oldest, still would have been too painful. Thankfully, his family understood this and were glad to share that day with us. I'm sure not all bereaved parents would feel as we did, but if your bereaved family member had an "only child," it would be best to check with him about family gatherings. Instead of a birthday gift for the mother or father of the deceased child, I suggest a donation in memory of the child or flowers taken to the cemetery.

Memorial Day, July 4th and Labor Day were difficult holidays as well because those long weekends had been spent in the past on our boat at a nearby lake with Molly and her friends. There are many things to be done to a boat in preparation for the summer months. Larry and I could not handle those preparatory tasks that first summer, so special friends did it all for us without our prior knowledge. They even towed the boat to the lake for us. All we had to do was show up! As these friends also moored their boat at the same lake, they planned their first trip to coincide with ours, knowing that the first time might be very sad for us. And, by the way, it was.

As previously mentioned, Molly's birthday was spent with special friends of ours and hers. Molly would have been 20 years old that October. Her previous birthday was spent at Arizona State University, which was also Parent's Weekend. Larry and I flew to Tempe that year for a glorious weekend with Molly and her new college friends. The birthday after her death was devastating but, again, thanks to thoughtful, caring friends and family members, we managed to make it through the day.

As friends and family of the bereaved parents, understand that sometimes they do need to be alone. Larry and I went on a short trip over Thanksgiving. We had been told that it was advisable to do something different over the holidays, so we "ran away." Some of our friends were upset that we chose to leave, but it was the right thing for us to do. It may be for your bereaved friends, as well.

Christmas is not a day, but rather a season. It is long and painful for the bereaved parents. They only want the entire season to end quickly. Because we had no other children, we exchanged no gifts, had no tree and did not decorate the house as in past years.

As friends, your understanding of their feelings is most important. The bereaved parents most likely will not wish to attend holiday parties, for there really is no joy in their hearts. As we've only been through the first Christmas without Molly, I do not know how we will handle this holiday in the future. "Alive Alone," a group for bereaved parents who have lost "only children" or "all children," taught us that because we have no other children, we are not obligated to follow any past Christmas traditions. It is best perhaps for the bereaved family to go away if at all possible. For many, however, that may not be an option. As close friends or family members, offer the bereaved diversions from their normal holiday traditions. Suggestions might be: Switching Christmas Eve routines to Christmas Day and vice versa; eating Christmas dinner at a restaurant instead of at home; plan a hiking or camping trip nearby; organize a special tribute for the deceased child by having other loved ones write a special memory, poem or prayer.

In our case, friends offered us their condo in California, so Larry and I left on December 20th for a two week road trip and did not return to Boulder until January 3, 1992. Friends with whom we had shared Christmas brunch for many years joined us in California. They, along with their two adult children, our godchildren, felt as we did about having a traditional Christmas celebration the first Christmas after Molly's death. It was too painful for them, as well. The warm days of California made Christmas quite different for all of us. We left behind the cold and snow of beautiful Colorado which in the past had given us such wonderful memories. We were very appreciative to be away from home that first Christmas, but even more appreciative not to be alone. When we arrived home, the horrible holidays were over, as well as 1991, the worst year of our lives.

We had been told that the two most difficult days of grief especially in that first year are the anniversaries of the child's birth and death. A friend whose child is also deceased, as well as our local Hospice organization, advised us to be out of town, if possible, on the day of Molly's anniversary date. If the bereaved parents are away from home, they will be less likely to re-live each moment of the terrible day. Even after being told this, Larry and I did not feel that it would be necessary. We felt that we had already been through and survived the hardest times—the Christmas holidays and her birthday. However, as the date of her death approached, the reality and memories of the previous year began to take its toll. We truly were not prepared for its pain and the overwhelming depression that engulfed us. The sadness seemed to take over our every thought. Our sleep was once again disturbed—our appetites diminished. We then thanked God for the advice to go away. A trip that had previously been planned with friends from California for my 50th birthday in February was delayed until March to coincide with the anniversary date of Molly's death. Our friends were wonderful and understood our pain. They kept us occupied and yet gave us time alone. The bereaved parents can never leave their pain behind, but friends can certainly help to distract them from constantly thinking of that most horrible day.

CHAPTER SIX

Fathers—what they need and normally do not receive

Men seldom communicate their feelings. They believe it is not masculine to cry. Many have been brought up in homes where love and affection are not openly displayed.

What happens to these men when their child, their own flesh and blood, dies before they do? They are not "supposed" to cry; they don't know how to express their pain and grief, but they need, more than anything, love and affection. Their sorrow and sadness is as great as the mother's, but few recognize or acknowledge it.

A father usually returns as quickly as possible to his job. It is easier *not* to deal with it there. He goes home in the evening to his wife and tries lovingly to help ease her pain, drying her tears, concerned and worried that he might lose her as well. He feels he must take care of her. In the process, the bereaved father does not take time for his own grief. Delaying the grieving process is very common for the father who returns to work, but it is not considered to be emotionally healthy.

As my husband, Larry, had not previously lost anyone close to him, Molly's death was overwhelming. His shock and disbelief lasted for several weeks. His state of shock fooled a lot of people. They thought he was very strong and "had it all together." Little did most of them know that he had not begun to face the awful reality of what had happened. In fact, in February, the month before the one year anniversary of Molly's death, Larry suddenly revealed his fear that he had never truly dealt with her death.

After he returned to work, business associates would ask him, "How's Linda doing?" They did not ask, "How are *you* doing?" Finally, one day he mentioned this to me with tears in his eyes.

He desperately wanted someone to talk with him about *his* pain, *his* grief, *his* love for our daughter. He needed to talk with someone besides me, but most of his male friends were too afraid to ask how he was for fear that they might not be able to handle his probable emotional response. Therefore, for most of his male business associates and friends, it was far easier to ask about me.

As a male or female friend, what can you do for the father? Understand that his needs are as great as the mother's. Take him to lunch and talk. Let him talk and express himself—let him cry. Listen to him. Cry with him. In your normal, busy life, take time for your bereaved friend. Call him on the phone during the day. Let him know you're thinking of him. Exercise with him. Play golf with him. Let him know he is loved and cared about.

There are many creative ways to be helpful, as this example proved to us: While Larry was still in a terrible state of shock upon returning to work, a thoughtful friend drove him to his office in Denver, waited a few hours, and then brought him home. What a wonderful and unselfish act of love! This continued for the first three or four days, and then Larry was capable of making the drive alone.

If your association with the bereaved father is in the work place, your friendship and help will be most needed and appreciated. Concentration and comprehension are almost impossible in the first months following the death of a child. Larry's co-workers understood this fact and relieved him of as much responsibility as possible. Without their loving assistance and concern, Larry might well have lost his job.

The sooner one begins the grieving process, the better it is for that person in the long run; however, it is never too late to begin. As mentioned before, a journal for the father is a wonderful gift. Writing a page or two in a journal takes very little time, but helps so much to alleviate some of the pain and sadness within the heart. The gift of a journal early on will assist the father in beginning the grieving process.

As a friend, also realize that your friend's grief is going to last a long time. Granted, he will be more like himself in the months ahead, but he will mourn his child for the rest of his life. He will never be the same person you once knew, but he will always be your friend. Don't be afraid to bring up the deceased child's name in the weeks, months and even years ahead, for your friend will greatly appreciate it. Talk about the good times and the memories you both share of the child. Remember, his child will never be far from his mind or his heart.

CHAPTER SEVEN

Teenage and young adult peers—how can you help?

If you are a friend of a teenager or a young adult who has died, you can be of tremendous help to the bereaved parents. You are a part of the child that is gone forever. The bereaved parents have lost their child, and they do not want to lose you. Because you are young, you will eventually drift into your own future, and rightly so. However, at this moment, you are in great pain suffering the loss of a dear friend. You perhaps need the companionship of the bereaved parents as much as they need you.

Molly's friends have previously been mentioned many times in this book, but more needs to be said.

I remember the day, the afternoon, the moment, that Molly's death had been confirmed. Earlier in the day, we were informed that she was missing. By the time her death was a certainty, one of her dearest friends was already at our home. He considered Molly his family— his sister—his best friend. Though his shock and pain were apparent, he immediately went to his home and began to notify Molly's other friends. Though many were students in Boulder at the University of Colorado, many more were scattered around the country. He and the other local friends made many calls spreading the word of our Molly's death. An hour or so later, the close friends came to our home. They sat with Larry and me in Molly's bedroom, holding each other and crying without speaking. Molly loved each of her friends so very much. All of them had been a part of our lives for a long time and we needed to be together on that most terrible of all days.

Starting the next day and continuing through the week, her friends arrived from around the country, as well as Canada and Australia. Each of them came to our home expressing their love for Molly and for us. Larry and I are still overwhelmed with their obvious devotion to Molly and their sincere concern for us. They were all here on and off throughout the week preceding the funeral.

Larry and I felt that these wonderful friends should be a part of Molly's service, as they were such an important part of her life. We asked if they would like to speak at the service and they gladly accepted. These young people had a planned meeting and organized their part of the service; and it was beautifully done. One friend who had attended grade school with Molly was asked to sing at the service. Everyone in the church was so touched by the love in her voice as she sang "Memories" and "Wind Beneath My Wings." Many commented that they were awed by her composure and ability to give this final gift of love to Molly. The Arizona State friends also formed together for their contribution to the service. The minister made an announcement that if anyone else wished to speak, they could come forward to the podium. More young friends, including cousins, gave their messages of love and sorrow.

Because Molly died during spring break vacation, many students at Arizona State did not learn of her death until they returned to school. Therefore, Molly's close friends organized a beautiful memorial service held at the chapel on campus three weeks after her death. They asked us to be present, if at all possible, and we agreed to do so. Though it was extremely difficult for us to return to the school where she had been so happy only a month before, it was rewarding for us to meet and talk with so many of her friends. The memorial itself was well planned with printed programs and a campus priest in charge of the services. Friends, as well as an Arizona State administrator, spoke about Molly and the tragedy of her death. Afterwards, we assembled outside where a compact disk player was playing Molly's favorite songs. Balloons were once again passed out and released. If you should be a college friend of the deceased child, this type of memorial service would be a wonderful tribute. I should mention also that the entire expense was covered by donations from friends in her dorm.

As peers of the deceased friend, keep in touch with the bereaved parents. We received, after Molly's friends returned to their various colleges, some of the most beautiful letters and cards. We shall keep them for the rest of our lives. Many of them phoned us regularly to let us know that we were in their thoughts and prayers.

Eleven of her friends decided they would like a special tribute to Molly at the cemetery. With our permission, they placed a small flat headstone in front of the stone Larry and I had purchased. Inscribed on it are lines from a song, "Written in Stone," by Randy Travis—"It's written in stone how I feel about you. It's written in stone what I want to do. Spend this life and the life hereafter loving you." Along with Molly's name are the names of her eleven friends who gave their last special gift of love to our daughter.

As previously mentioned, Molly's friends did not forget us on Mother's Day, Father's Day, Larry's birthday, Molly's birthday or the other holidays. The friends here in Boulder, of course, were around the most on these occasions. The others in out-of-state colleges made a point to stop by and spend time with us when they were home on vacations.

During Thanksgiving break and Christmas break, many of them asked to be together in our home. On these special occasions, I would either fix dinner or they would bring dinner to us. We sat together after dinner and discussed everyone's lives, but most of all, we talked about Molly. They talked and laughed about their memories of her. They also discussed their pain and grief, and cried openly for their missing friend.

It has been more than a year now since Molly's death, and we still are in contact with most of her closest friends. They still call, write, have dinner with us and remember the special occasions that are difficult for all of us. Larry and I are well aware that this will not go on forever, as they are young and have their whole lives ahead of them. We do believe, however, that some of her friends will always remain close.

As friends of the deceased child, you should be aware that many of Molly's friends required counseling the summer after her death. Some went as a group to our local Hospice organization. Others found individual counseling helpful. You need to understand and be prepared for all the ups and downs of grieving. You will experience many of the same symptoms and problems that the bereaved parents experience.

Do not be afraid to cry with the bereaved parents, for your tears are healthy and a must for your own recovery.

CHAPTER EIGHT

Understanding the bereaved parent

Your friends, the parents of the now deceased child, are entering into the worst experience of their lives. This is not to say that they will not ever feel joy again or have happy times, for they will. But for the duration of their existence, there will be an emptiness inside their hearts that no one can ever fill.

You must understand from the beginning that, try as you may, you *cannot* take away the pain of your grieving friends. The pain of loss is to be with them for the rest of their lives. Only time, struggle and the desire to live again can ease this pain in the years to come. One of the best cards Larry and I received was from a very sensitive and intelligent friend, for the card simply stated, "If it hurts you to look back, frightens you to look ahead, then just look beside you...I'll be there."

Following are characteristics and problems that your bereaved friends will experience immediately after the death of their child.

1. *Loss or Gain of Appetite and Weight.* I remember so well our friends trying to make sure that Larry and I were getting something into our stomachs. I personally had trouble swallowing. It was as though the food would get stuck in my throat. Friends thoughtfully cut everything into small bite-size pieces. Larry and I both lost a considerable amount of weight. However, some people react to grief in just the opposite way and eating can become obsessive.

2. *Lack of Comprehension and Concentration.* From the beginning and for a very long time afterward, your bereaved friends will

have a difficult time comprehending conversations going on around them. Realize their attention span will be very short. We both had trouble comprehending anything we read for quite a while.

3. *Physical Problems.* Depression makes one very tired. Getting up in the morning and showering was a major feat for us. In the first week, I barely had enough energy to stand up after sitting any length of time. Many times we felt dizzy and weak from the lack of physical strength and energy. I would like to state also that I entered menopause shortly after Molly's death. Though my age contributed, I believe the shock of Molly's death escalated the timing.

4. *Sleep Problems.* With the help of tranquilizers, Larry and I were able to catch a little sleep each night. Even with the medication though, sleep did not come easily. Larry required medication for three weeks, while I stopped using anything after one week. It will be different for each person. (I should note here that a friend's hot tub for just three nights was the solution to end Larry's need for medication.) For many weeks, we both suffered extreme hot flashes during the night, waking up drenched in perspiration. As badly as your bereaved friends need their rest, there will be few quality hours of sleep.

5. *The Pain of Grief.* The bereaved parents will feel pain like they have never experienced before. It feels like a knife cutting through their very hearts and souls. They perhaps will try to describe this pain to you but will be unable to adequately do so. They will want this awful pain to go away, but it will not for quite some time.

6. *TV, Newspapers and Radio.* We had no interest in any of these things for a long time. Not only is concentration a problem as previously mentioned, but bereaved parents cannot and probably should not deal with other problems of the world at this time. They truly will have little or no interest in what is going on around them. They can barely make it through each day handling their own grief. Songs played on the radio can be devastating to the bereaved. So many songs will remind them of their child, of happier times and of future times that can never be. Most of the time, my husband and I now listen to talk shows on the car radio.

7. *Fear of the Future.* Try not to talk of future times or specific dates with your bereaved friends, for the future is so frightening for

them. It will seem as though there can be no future for them without their child in it. The bereaved parents must learn to live one day at a time, for it is the only way they can survive the first few months.

8. *Phone Calls.* Don't be surprised if your bereaved friends do not return your phone calls immediately. There will be days when they simply cannot respond to people. There will be days when they must be alone. If your bereaved friends do not have an answering machine, suggest they buy one or go together and give it as a gift.

9. *Religious Beliefs.* If your friends have previously been religiously inclined, do not be surprised if they now question or doubt their prior beliefs. They may be very angry at God and find themselves rejecting him when they need him most. This feeling of anger against their own beliefs may go on for quite some time. Don't criticize them. Pray for them and hope that their religion can once again give them the peace and support they so desperately need.

In the weeks and months ahead, your bereaved friends will encounter many side-effects of their grief.

1. *Emotions.* The bereaved will not always be able to control their emotions, particularly in public. One minute they feel things are going rather well, then a song is played, or someone says something that triggers a memory, or a well-meaning person appears with verbal condolences. Once the tears begin, it is difficult to cut them off. Many times, the bereaved finds it necessary to leave the restaurant, movie theater or other public place. One night we saw a young lady walking with some of her friends who very closely resembled our Molly. The shock of the experience ruined our entire evening.

2. *Memory Loss.* Friends of ours who had lost their son several years previous to Molly's death, warned us that it would often feel as though our brains had been damaged from the grief and pain. Larry and I found this to be true in many aspects of our lives. For example, I had shopped at the same grocery store for eighteen years, but on my first trip alone, I honestly could not remember where anything was located. I left in tears, mostly out of frustration and also a feeling of embarrassment. Cooking was another problem for me. Favorite recipes had to be re-learned and cooking utensils had to be searched for in a familiar kitchen.

Therefore, don't be surprised if your bereaved friends have a difficult time remembering people's names, events of the past, or even things they used to do so well.

3. *Socializing.* As previously mentioned, socializing will be almost impossible for quite some time, except for small groups of special friends. Large parties given for any reason will probably not appeal to the bereaved parents. Going out to dinner with two or three other couples worked best for us. Having dinner with friends in their homes was also welcomed, for it afforded us the space and freedom to cry openly if necessary.

4. *Major Decisions.* Making decisions at all is difficult for the bereaved, but any major decisions should be put off for at least a year, according to grief experts. Changes in careers, selling a house, or moving out-of-state should be postponed until the bereaved are more stable and in better physical condition. They will need the support of their friends and family for a long time.

In closing this chapter, I would just like to remind you to be patient with your bereaved friends. The road back to living is slow, and for each person, the time involved in recovery will be different. There are no rules to determine any one person's allotment of time for grieving.

CHAPTER NINE

Things to say—and not to say to newly bereaved parents

Though the bereaved parents will know and understand what you do say is coming from your love and concern for them, be aware that some things are better left unsaid. There are also some comments that might be appropriate and consoling later on, when the bereaved parents are more responsive.

DO NOT SAY

1. *It must have been God's will.* Why would God want their child to die?

2. *God must have needed your child.* No one needs the child more than the bereaved parents.

3. *I understand how you feel.* You cannot know how they feel unless you also have lost a child. A loss of a loved one is always devastating, whether it be a parent, a spouse, a cousin, a grandparent or a good friend. Having lost both my mother and father eight months apart when I was in my early twenties, I felt sure nothing could ever cause me as much pain again. I was wrong. The pain of losing my child was somehow deeper and more intense than anyone can imagine or describe. Therefore, do not make a comparison of any past losses to your bereaved friends, for no loss truly is as great as that of one's own child.

4. *He or she is in a better place now.* Unless the deceased child was gravely ill, the parents will resent this comment because they feel their child was happy where he or she was.

5. *You have so many wonderful memories.* In the beginning of grief, the memories will only hurt the bereaved parents. They also know there will be no future memories to make with that child.

6. *(Name of child) wants you to be happy and go on with your lives.* At this time, the parents have not a clue how to be happy, much less how they are going to continue their lives without their beloved child.

7. *Time heals all wounds.* Time cannot heal a broken heart—not when a child dies. Time will eventually help—but cannot heal.

8. *You are a strong person.* A bereaved parent is not a strong person. Never before has he felt more fragile and weak. Hopefully, he will be strong again in the future, but not now.

9. *Don't spend too much money on the funeral or the headstone.* Though this is probably good advice, be careful. Remember—this is the last gift the bereaved parents can give to their child.

10. *It's time to move on.* There is no specific time frame for an individual to grieve. Everyone is different. Grieving for a child is a lifelong ordeal for most. Gradually, the bereaved parents will indeed move on, but one step at a time, and only when they are ready and capable of doing so.

THINGS TO SAY

The following are words of great comfort and sensitivity. They speak for themselves.

1. I love you.
2. I cannot begin to understand your pain, but I'm here for you.
3. Would you like to talk?
4. I loved your child and miss him/her.
5. We'll get through this together.
6. I know your pain will last forever, but I want to help.
7. I'm praying for you every day.
8. You will all be together someday.
9. (Name of child) loved you so much.
10. You were the best parent/parents.
11. I'm proud of you.
12. May God bless you and give you strength.

CHAPTER TEN

As a friend, remember to take care of yourself

As a friend of the bereaved parents, you will play a very important part in their recovery. However, you must not forget that you, as a friend, also are suffering the pain of grief, not only for the child that is now gone, but for your dear friend.

If you are a friend who is very close to the bereaved parents and/or to the now deceased child, you should expect to experience many of the same problems as the bereaved parents, such as memory and concentration loss, loss of appetite and control of one's emotions.

Molly's friends who returned to their college classes after her funeral all had a difficult time concentrating on various subject matters. Everything seemed so meaningless to them. After the summer break, the fall semester was easier for most of them, but being in control of their emotions was still a problem. They could not and still cannot predict when the tears of sadness will fall.

In other words, be aware that you are very normal if you go through any or all of the same characteristics as the bereaved parents. Some of you may require therapy whether with a bereavement group, a minister, or private consultation with a psychologist or psychiatrist.

Some of our friends read grief books so that they could better understand us and what we were going through. I strongly suggest that you do the same, as many of the books will help you to better understand yourself and your own pain.

For your own benefit, take care of yourself. Get as much sleep and rest as possible. Eat balanced meals and watch your alcohol and drug consumption. During the time prior to the funeral, you may want to be at the bereaved parents' home all of the time because you feel that you are needed. And granted, you are needed, but you must allow yourself time away each day from the hectic activity and from the overwhelming grief. You will need time alone, as well as time with your own family. Other friends can fill in when you are not there—remember that everyone wants to help, so give them a chance to contribute. Organize time schedules with friends so that you can have the free time you desperately need.

At some given time after the funeral, whether it be two or three weeks or two months, try to get away for a short or even long vacation. You will need to do this for your own sanity. Though you love your bereaved friends dearly, you need a break from the pain and sadness. Their pain can consume you, leaving you with nothing to give to your own family. You will become extremely frustrated when you finally realize that no matter what you do, you cannot eliminate their horrible depression. When you leave, God knows you will take their pain with you, but different surroundings can help you to relax and have personal moments of happiness and laughter.

Last, but certainly not least, remember that your bereaved friends love and cherish you. Your loving support, understanding and patience will never be forgotten.

A PRAYER

It is my joy in life to find
At every turning of the road
The strong arm of a comrade kind
To help me onward with my load.
And since I have no gold to give,
and love alone must make amends,
My only prayer is, while I live—
God make me worthy of my friends.

Frank Dempster Sherman

EPILOGUE. FIVE YEARS LATER

Since the first publication of "I Don't Know How To Help Them," Larry and I have continued to be supported by many of our friends, family members and Molly's friends.

In March of this year, Molly will have been deceased five years. She is still in our thoughts daily, and most definitely, in our hearts forever. There are still times of painful grief and tears, but not as often now. The loving memories of our days together are precious, and we are grateful that God entrusted her care to us while she was here. Her death has changed our lives, but because of the love and support of friends and family, we are once again functioning human beings.

The continued support has come in many forms but mostly from phone calls and letters during the difficult times of the year—Thanksgiving, Christmas, Molly's birthday and the anniversary date of her death.

Molly's friends continue to spend time with us throughout the year. Their visits, though not as often as the first couple of years, are very special times for Larry and me. We appreciate and love each of them more than words can say. Most of them have graduated from college now, two are engaged to be married, and others are having exciting lives in the business world. We believe each of them are taking Molly along into their new worlds of activity, and she will always be a part of their lives.

Larry and I are extremely grateful to our families for their patience and understanding. They realize, though time has indeed lessened the intensity of our pain, the pain of losing Molly will always exist for us.

My second book, "Standing Beside You," was published in January of 1996. This book was written for bereaved parents to not only give them information—but to give them *hope* and *encouragement* for the months and years ahead of them.

As friends and family members of bereaved parents, I urge you to give them unconditional love forever and to accept them as the new people they have become. Remember—they did not ask for this to happen to them. If they could turn back the clock and reverse their horrible fate, they would. Take them flowers, write a note, make a phone call just to say you are thinking of them. Take a trinket or a stuffed animal to their child's grave with your name on it, or even leave a business card. What may seem trivial to you will be monumentally important to the parents or parent of the child who is now gone from their loving embrace.

God bless each and every one of you who care enough to read this book, for you are the unselfish and loving people who can make a difference to a bereaved parent struggling to survive.

Linda K. Maurer

BEREAVEMENT GROUPS

Alive Alone, Inc.
11115 Dull Robinson Road
Van Wert, OH 45891

Literature distributed by *Alive Alone, Inc.*, describes itself as "a nonprofit corporation organized for such educational and charitable purposes as will benefit bereaved parents whose only child or all children are deceased, by providing a self-help network and publications to promote communication and healing, to assist in resolving their grief, and a means to reinvest their lives for a positive future."

American Self-Help Clearinghouse
201-625-7101

For listings and directories in finding or forming mutual aid self-help group.

Association for Death Education and Counseling (ADEC)
638 Prospect Avenue
Hartford, CT 06105-4298

Bereavement Magazine
8133 Telegraph Drive
Colorado Springs, CO 80920

A magazine of hope and healing.

Bereavement Support Group Program for Children
Participant Workbook and Leader Manual
Accelerated Development, Inc., Publishers
3400 Kilgore Avenue
Muncie, IN 47304-4896
317-284-4896

Bereavement Support Program
Caledonia Home Health Care
PO Box 383
St. Johnsbury, VT 05819
802-748-8116

Learning about grief—a guide to group discussions with children.

Camp Hope Helping Others Pain End
816 2nd Street N
Stevens Point, WI 54481
715-341-0076

A camp for grieving children.

Center for Loss and Grief Therapy
Linda Goldman, MS
Co-Director Ellen Zinner, PsyD
10400 Connecticut Avenue, Suite 514
Kensington, MD 20895-3944
301-942-6440

Provides counseling and support services for grieving adults, children, and perinatal loss.

Center for Loss and Life Transition
Dr. Alan Wolfelt
3735 Broken Bow Road
Ft. Collins, CO 80526
303-226-6050

Center for Loss in Multiple Birth (Climb, Inc.)
Jeane Kollantai
PO Box 1064
Palmer, AK 99645

Support group by and for parents who have experienced the death of one, both, or all of their children during a twin or higher multiple pregnancy, at birth or in infancy.

Includes parents who have undergone selective reduction as well as parents who have learned that one twin has serious anomalies. Wonderful resource organization for parents.

Centering Corporation
1531 North Saddle Creek Road
Omaha, Nebraska 68104-5064
402-553-1200

Bereavement Publishing Company. Write or call for catalog.

Children and Grief Hospice of North Carolina, Inc.
1046 Washington Street
Raleigh, NC 27605

Lesson plans included for all ages.

The Compassionate Friends
P. O. Box 3696
Oak Brook, IL 60522-3696

The *Compassionate Friends'* newsletter states that this group is a "mutual assistance self-help organization offering friendship and understanding to bereaved parents and siblings. The primary purpose is to assist them in the positive resolution of the grief experienced upon the death of a child and to support their efforts to achieve physical and emotional health."

Education Programs Associates
Customer Service
1 W Campbell Avenue, Bldg. D, Room 40
Campbell, CA 95008
617-232-8390

Good Grief: Helping groups of children when a friend dies.
Sandra Sutherland Fox
ACSW Judge Baker Children's Center
295 Longwood Avenue
Boston, MA 02115
617-232-8390

Ms. Fox includes several books that provide a comprehensive view of providing services for grieving children which includes information for schools and individuals. Includes cultural and ethnic differences. She has developed and includes an extensive bibliography in her books.

Grief Counseling and Support Center of Hospice of
Winston-Salem/Forsyth County, Inc.
1100-C South Stratford Road, Suite 201
Winston-Salem, NC 27103
919-768-3972
FAX 919-659-0461

Support groups and counseling.

H.A.N.D. (Helping After Neonatal Death)
PO Box 341 Los Gatos, CA 95031
408-732-3228

Resource network for information concerning pregnancy loss and neonatal death. Resource library, phone support, peer support groups, inservice programs, newsletter.

Heartbeat
2956 S. Wolff Street
Denver, CO 80236
303-934-8464

Self-help support group for survivors of suicide. Facilitors are not professional, but all survivors.

Hope for Bereaved, Inc. Support Groups and Services
4500 Onodaga Boulevard
Syracuse, NY 13219
315-475-9675

Support groups and services, listening, counseling, and referrals. Also, telephone helpline: 315-475-HOPE (4673). These two publications are available through them: *Hope for Bereaved: Understanding, Coping and Growing Through Grief; How to Form Support Groups and Services for Grieving People.*

Human Services Press
PO Box 2423
Springfield, IL 62705
217-258-1756

Books, audio cassettes (self-help).

IN LOVING MEMORY
1416 Green Run Lane
Reston,Virginia 22090
703-435-0608

Dedicated to helping parents cope with the death of their only child or all children.

Kinder Mourn
515 Fenton Place
Charlotte, NC 28207
704-376-2580

The purpose of Kinder Mourn is to assist professionals in working with bereaved families and educating the community regarding parental and sibling grief.

LARGO
1192 S. Uvald Street
Aurora, Colorado 80012

Largo is a quarterly newsletter for parents who have had more than one child die.

Minnesota Sudden Infant Death Center
Minneapolis Children's Medical Center
2525 Chicago Avenue South
Minneapolis, MN 55404
612-0863-6285

National Hospice Organization
1901 North Moore Street
Suite 901
Arlington, VA 2220

National Self-Help Clearinghouse
212-642-2944

For listings and directories in finding or forming a mutual self-help group.

Parents of Murdered Children
National Headquarters
100 E. 8th Street
Cincinnati, OH 45202 (513-721-5683)
Colorado State Coordinator: 303-722-6004

Penny for Pines
National Forest Service
900 West Grand Avenue
Porterville, CA 93257-2035

For donating $60 to the National Forest Service for tree replacement, you will receive a memorial plaque engraved with your child's name.

Pen-Parents
PO Box 8738
Reno, NV 89507-8738

Pen-Parents is a support network which provides an opportunity for bereaved parents to talk about their loss through correspondence with others in similar situations. Good resource for parents who have interrupted pregnancies.

Pregnancy and Infant Loss Center
1421 East Wayzata Boulevard
Suite 40
Wayzata, MN 55391

Non-profit organization offering support, resources, and education on miscarriage, stillbirth, and infant death.

SHARE Pregnancy and Infant Loss Support, Inc.
National SHARE Office
St. Joseph Health Center
300 First Capitol Drive St.
Charles, Missouri 63301-2893
314-947-6164
FAX 314-947-7486

The mission of SHARE is to serve those who are touched by the tragic death of a baby through miscarriage, stillbirth, or newborn death.

BEREAVEMENT BOOKS

Some of the below-listed books were given to us by friends or by Reverend John Hess. We purchased some of them ourselves in local bookstores. Your friends may not relate to each and every book listed, but hopefully some of the books or at least portions of some of the books will help your bereaved friends find some peace and strength for the future.

Dunn, Paul H. and Richard M. Eyre, *The Birth that We Call Death*. (A book for anyone who has lost a loved one.)

Hackett, Don and Kay Bevington, *Now Childless*. (For parents who have lost their only child.)

Heavilin, Marilyn Willett, *Roses in December*. (The author writes of the deaths of her three sons.)

Hickman, Martha Whitmore, *I Will Not Leave You Desolate*. (Written by a mother who lost her daughter in a fall from a horse.)

Holmes, Marjorie, *To Help You Through the Hurting*. (For anyone who has lost a loved one.)

Knapp, Ronald J., *Beyond Endurance — When a Child Dies*. (Dr. Knapp interviewed 155 families who experienced the death of a child. He examines three types of death: death occurring after a long illness, sudden or unexpected death, and death by murder.)

Kushner, Rabbi Harold S., *Why Bad Things Happen to Good People*.

Moody, Raymond A., *Life After Life*. (Concerning near-death experiences.)

Moody, Raymond A., *The Light Beyond*. (Concerning near-death experiences.)

Morse, Melvin, M.D., *Closer to the Light*. (Concerning near-death experiences of children.)

Osgood, Judy, *Meditations for Bereaved Parents*. (Thirty-five mothers and fathers share their anger and their anguish, but even more important, they share the insights that have enabled them to heal, to reinvest in living, to smile and love again.)

Osmont, Kelly and Marilyn McFarlane, *Parting Is Not Goodbye ... Coping with Grief in Creative, Healthy Ways*. (A single parent, Kelly Osmont tells of the death of her only child.)

Price, Eugenia, *Getting Through the Night*. (For anyone who has lost a loved one.)

Schiff, Harriet Sarnoff, *The Bereaved Parent*. (Written by a mother who lost her son.)

Wolterstorff, Nicholas, *Lament for a Son*. (The author writes of his personal grief when his son dies in a mountain-climbing accident.)

About the Author

Linda was born and raised in Indianapolis, Indiana. Her parents, Karl and Molly Kramer, died in 1968. She has one brother, Michael W. Kramer, who lives in Longmont, Colorado.

She and her husband, Larry, were married in 1969 and reside in Boulder, Colorado.

Molly Marie, their only child, was born October 13, 1971 and died on March 16, 1991.

Her second book titled "Standing Beside You" was published in January, 1996.

NOTES

NOTES

<u>N</u>OTES

NOTES